FIRST STEPS

Overcoming Early Obstacles to Recovery from Abuse

T. Pitt Green

No Substitute for Appropriate Care

This work is not a substitute for medical or mental health care interventions or protocol. The contents of this work are based solely on personal experiences of the authors and are intended to advance understanding and public dialogue only. Nothing in this book is a recommendation or seeks to promote a specific method, approach, diagnosis, or treatment as is reserved to the proper purview of physicians, specialists, and mental health care professionals. The authors are not engaged in rendering legal, medical, psychological, or financial counsel and make no representations or warranties thereto. If expert assistance is required or wished for, the counsel of a professional should be sought.

If you or someone you love is in urgent need of assistance or in crisis, dial 911 to ask for immediate help or to go a local medical care facility.

Permissions Required

Scripture Citations

Along the Via Dolorosa, Jesus was dragging his Cross—and our redemption—on the torn flesh of his abused and wounded body. Veronica slipped out of the crowd to wipe His face with a moist cloth. The image He gave her was formed in blood and dirt and sweat. She beheld that image with her broken heart and saw beauty.

PREFACE

This book is a selection of my reflections about a mystifying watershed in the lives of many survivors of sexual and other abuse: when the past finally catches up to the present, and life takes an unexpected turn.

Some reflections are drawn from *Veronica's Veil: A Christ-Centered Guide for Integrating Faith with Recovery for Adult Survivors of Child Sexual Abuse by Clergy*, which I co-authored with Fr. Lou Fiorelli, OSFS. Published in 2014, *Veronica's Veil* promotes knowledgeable and sensitive spiritual support for adults who are healing from abuse in a faith setting and for those who are exploring how to integrate their Christian faith—and the great treasury found in Catholic Tradition and devotions—into recovering from sexual and other abuse.

Having become a go-to reference for many, *Veronica's Veil* was recognized by Cabrini University's *Cors Jesu* Award for furthering the cause of social justice.

Fr. Lou and I offered retreats and workshops where topics in *Veronica's Veil* were developed over several years. Writing the book was a way to share more broadly what our small groups found edifying and healing. Readers appreciated the deep dive into elements of pastoral ministry to survivors, but they noted that survivors and their family members needed something briefer that focused on just a survivor's day-to-day experience. I began to distribute photocopied selections to event attendees. Eventually certain survivor essays stood out as favorites. To these, I added original reflections about the strange phase of recovery when we are being driven out of a comfort zone and into transformation. The resulting collection is this little book, which is intended for people—survivors and family members—who are immersed in a process of healing from abuse and who are exploring how our faith can support recovery.

In fact, four little books have been similarly compiled, starting with this one, *First Steps*. They each address an important aspect of recovering from abuse, such as turning points which define us. I hope you find one that is focused on whatever challenge you face—or someone you love faces—today.

CONTENTS

THE BEGINNING

It all begins when life stops working. Life stops working in different ways for different people, but there is no doubt that what has been familiar starts to feel strange.

What creates this shift may be an obvious catalyst, or there may be nothing particular to see, just a shocking shift in perspective. There may be a crisis that captures our focus, such as a dramatic life change, but that shift, however extreme, may turn out to be nothing more than a sign of some deeper upheaval which we will understand only in retrospect, possibly years later. What is certain, however, whether it is ushered in as a personal cataclysm or slow-motion burn of misery, it is the end of life as we expected it to be.

The beginning sets into motion something deeper and, for much time, something difficult to see. The beginning is more like the swarm of earthquakes and other subterranean disturbances which geologists meticulously study, hoping to identify when magma will erupt from the depth of the earth and make its escape into air and sea. The beginning is the end of pressure building up over a very long period of time—since the first strike of the abuse, when the agony was buried with the memories, lest they destroy the victim. From the moment this buried firestorm of feelings and memories begins its pathway up through the resistance of rock and sediment, we are likely to find no peace or relief until what burns deep within us is released.

WARRIOR'S CONUNDRUM

One way life stops working is that the battlefield shifts. We used to know the rules of the warrior and, especially because we were survivors, had mastered an impressive range of defensive (and sometimes offensive) skills, but when it all begins we start to notice the rules on which we relied now apply less and the skills give us no advantage. We stand disoriented in the smoldering field feeling some overwhelming issue to which we should be impervious. But we no longer feel any safety from the onslaught of this unknown thing.

This means we have come to the end of our defenses. These are old defenses. They have become out-dated. It's about to become a problem that they are well-rooted and highly practiced.

They are second-nature. They have been the cornerstone in our approach to the world and can seem to others like facets of our personality. But there comes a point in our later life when we realize these champion's defenses simply have lost their utility.

These defenses represent our brilliance in surviving danger when we had no other options. We developed defenses to survive the abuse. Our defenses were all about the abuser being on the offensive. Our defenses had one goal: to preserve our welfare as much as possible using our own very, very limited power over what was happening to us. For most of us, there was no power to stop the abuser, but our defenses helped us endure the abuse and to survive in some way. But defenses show what we needed to do to survive. One way is that they can be seen to have preserved the abuse in secrecy. We will pay for that silence every moment until we can share the experience, but we had to survive first, before we could be somewhere safe enough to heal.

Thanks to our defenses we were able to live and function to some degree in a dangerous situation. In fact, our defenses were a creative response, ingenious really, to finding ourselves in a perilous and vulnerable state, protected by no one, being abused.

Yet life goes on. At some point, our lives outgrow those valuable defenses. We may move away from the abuser, or the abuser may die or grow too old to fear. We may find ourselves in other dangerous settings but are constrained by old habits accustomed to abuse. You see, the defenses may have improved levels of safety while abuse was actively underway, but they also encoded an identity of being a victim in how we react to the world.

We are getting older. Simply with time, the world around us is changing. Our defenses no longer match the circumstances. They no longer provide what we need because what we need has changed. Even if the abuser is still in our lives—on the margins or in some other way—they are aging. We are by circumstance safer, and the defenses we once needed now begin to work against our growth. They begin to constrain us. The way they program our reactions begins to interfere with better lives we are now living, or they serve to perpetuate unhealthy circumstances from which we need to be free.

We are like weary warriors, called to put down our armor before we can feel certain the battle is over and the war is won. The beginning drives us to believe. That leap of faith is all we have to lead us out of a forever memory state.

THE SPARK

The shift at the beginning proceeds with or without us. Often, we resist it. We reject the shift. We resent the changes. We deny the up-heaval. I did. Yet, somewhere deep inside, we are drawn to reject the constraints that hold us back. What creates such a tension of its own power?

It is as if, somewhere deep inside us, we are being animated by the idea of a more healed self. Why else would a status quo sacrifice itself? What other good could come of a surrender where there has only been conflict and peril?

The idea is not conscious, at first. If it were, why would we not recognize it right away? It is a memory of a wellness we might have had. It is an image of a well-self, who never came to be, buried with memories and feelings from when the abuser killed our innocence and potential and personality with the domination of our bodies. We likely do not even know this inchoate person exists within us. This person, who was strong enough to survive abuse, usually is reduced into a cringe of hurt and feels the loss of potential acutely, even when what it lost is just an intimation... a hint... a whiff of some better life. Sometimes people mistake that victims of abuse remember only the horror, but we also face memories of whom we might have been—and who we may yet become.

What, then, could preserve such a memory of a lost self, such a hope for escape from abuse that can last all these years? What can dare to dream of life? It is not by our own power that we can recall who we were created to be. But in recovering we can encounter that purpose all over again. We may discover this self over time, as we walk through recovery, or we may just recognize him or her instantly in a memory or in a new moment or experience now. What we can be sure is that this identity is there to be discovered, it is breaking through outdated defenses to come back to life. This is my experience: The beginning of my recovery was like being set on fire by a divine spark within me which abuse could not extinguish, and which came back from embers to full flame, drawing life from what is divine beyond me. That identity was forever changed by the experience of abuse and its aftermath, but I was not dead. I was a survivor.

With a divine spark growing within us, all it takes now is a catalyst to bring forward a full flame.

"The most courageous steps which a survivor will ever take are the first steps in the beginning of recovery."

THE CATALYST

No survivor volunteers to begin recovering from abuse. Who would? It is a daunting process, especially if viewed from the starting point. Most survivors believe anyway that they have left the abuse behind—or even have healed from the abuse. The abuse has been relegated to the past. We are usually somewhere else from the abuser or otherwise beyond peril under their authority. It's over. The abuse is past fact.

Memories of that time of life when abuse was active may even seem benign. The good times are what our memories emphasize, or embellish. The darker events may be wholly buried. They may be mostly buried, with the just the tip like an iceberg in view. Everything seems emotionally tidy. Life has gone on. Our days seem under

11

control. But then something shifts. Memories become radioactive with emotion. Our reactions to familiar things in daily life seem out of sorts. New and old situations start to create distress or fear. This is beginning.

What causes this shift to happen? The catalysts vary as widely as survivors and experiences of abuse vary.

Some common catalysts are related to public discussions of abusers. Survivors can feel free to speak of their own experience after news reports of an unknown abuser's conviction or after an exposé on abuse becomes part of conversations. Other survivors are drawn to share their own abuse experience when a friend or family member dares to divulge their own. Sometimes all we need is the permission to share. A door opens. We run through.

Most survivors hold back even when the public focus is on abuse. For these survivors, the catalyst is not clearly linked to abuse. Treatment for symptoms of depression or other mental illness often take a fresh look at our lives, including our past. In the process, we discover in memories, which we already consciously know, signs of abuse we do not remember. Recovery from other issues, such as addiction or cancer, creates a new level of vulnerability and launches a review of the past. Any life events can be catalysts. Victims of crime often re-experience past violence as well, whether or not a memory of abuse is conscious. A family funeral puts a survivor back in the same room as an abuser, and the painful memories wake up with new vigor. A divorce recreates disruption in safety within the home, bringing back to life the sense of fright and danger of being a child abused. A parent dies, so we no longer feel compelled to protect them with a secret, so we can start to talk about what was before kept locked away. Service in the military or as a first-responder exposes people to trauma, which in turn can rattle abuse memories from childhood. Women arrested find in law enforcement or a social worker the first compassionate witness who listens to their history of being trafficked, permitting them to see their own abuse began as a child in the home. Sometimes we have no idea that a catalyst has kicked off the beginning of the process of recovery—until years later, in retrospect.

Catalysts vary. Our reactions to catalysts vary. This is what happens in every case. The catalyst brings us to an excavation site, where we slowly, perhaps begrudgingly like me, realize something lies buried in darkness which must be brought into the Light. The meticulous work of sifting is ours alone to do. We need to set aside armor and defense for the tools of exploring the ruins left by abuse in our lives.

The Shift

There is nothing neat about the beginning. It is good to understand that there are catalysts for the beginning, but there is nothing orderly about catalysts or how recovery kicks off. There is seldom a single catalyst. There is seldom one specific beginning. Like many trickles leading to many rivulets leading to many rivers running through a single delta to the open sea, catalysts are of different magnitudes and power. The shift is when the waters start running where there has been only frozen grief. Anyone who has witnessed winter's ice cracking beneath a springtime sun can attest, the screeches and howls as frozen waterways break up offer up hints of wild wounded animals in nearby woods and of monstrous specters warning us against entry. The beginning can be like that, frightening, visited by ghosts we notice are familiar before we realize their appearances are not about death. The shift is messy.

In practical terms, what does the shift look like? Survivors describe the arrival of new or changed memories. For some, new but mystifying memory fragments start to cut into a conscious day; we have no idea what these startling daydreams mean, yet they persist. Other survivors wake with night sweats, rattled by images that are not easily dismissed as residue from a terrible day; we have no idea why our dreams are haunting us. Sometimes someone has urged us to get professional help because our life is falling apart, yet we can hardly imagine what there is to discuss as we see nothing seems to have recently changed. Or survivors often talk about being suddenly shaken or paralyzed by anxiety or irrational fears—or anger—but we have no idea why our emotions have become too strong to control. There are times when survivors move out of addiction and, in recovery, face what we had numbed with self-medication; facing that now, we are tempted to relapse. Simply put, we become uncomfortable in ways that often make no sense. Our lives have stopped working the way we are accustomed to life working.

The shift affects everything eventually. Work we loved in the past may be uncomfortable for us now. People who understood us before may not understand us at all. People who never understood us before now are more uncomfortable with us as we start to move toward our own understanding; this may sound odd, and it is odd, but it is often very true. If you think about it, however, that makes sense. We no longer understand ourselves. We are no longer comfortable in our own skin. The pressure will release with time. We find new orientation and understanding—and comfort—in time. But this process must run its course, and it may feel rocky at times.

17

This is all a normal part of a paradigm shift. How we organized our thought and feelings is being challenged. We need to rethink and re-feel and rebuild. This can leave interests and love and work and relationships intact, but it never leaves anything unchanged. In fact, it is a helluva mess for a while, but the hope is in the chaos not in the orderly life sitting on top of emotions and memories that are roiling like magma just waiting for an escape hatch.

FIRE AND ICE

Paradigm shifts will change how we think and what we think. When the paradigm for understanding our lives and the abuse shifts, it can feel like we do not know who we are, because often we denied the suffering half of ourselves. It can feel like our life is that of a stranger, because we have relationships and made decisions that ignored the suffering portion of ourselves. As we connect what is conscious in the present with what is buried in the past, we eventually become whole, but first we become very confused. The combination process is more like an interior conflict, a shifting of tectonic layers deeply below our daily lives. This was a time when, for me, poetry and writing helped step over the crumbling intellectual artifices I had built to contain the past from my waking days.

It helped me to create images that were shielded from my intellect and its overthinking. I needed to have some sense of where I stood as life shifted around me, and my brain was not helping. Early in the process, I found myself torn between images of fire and of ice. Eventually, I realized the shift in the beginning of my recovery was driven by both.

The ice floes were breaking up, and suggestions of all the grief that lay buried in me howled like echoes bouncing against all sorts of places and events for me. Yet, even while the past was disturbing me long before I had begun to grapple with its detail, there was inherent in these images—these nightmares sometimes—a sense of what should be. There was a sense of what could be—smoothly flowing currents with flourishing life on all the banks and within the pathways of grief.

And there was something burning within me

seeking its way out of the dark into the Light. Memories and old feelings like magma were forcing a pathway upward to release, shimmying through layers of sediment and resistance, creating quakes and shudders, sending forward inexplicable geysers of emotion. They were all so terribly unfamiliar with their aching for hope and healing of which I had despaired.

The fire burned, and the icy grief above it was breaking up. The heat and the quakes in the earth below were disturbing the frozen waters. A sun's warmth was bearing down from above. The battlefield, whose victim's hell had been numbed with an extinguished fire and frozen waters, was coming back to life. It was impossible to be sure the battle would not resume, yet the reliable defenses were misfiring. It was a frightening time. I was disoriented, even humiliated, by the stubborn gap between what I wanted and what I was doing.

"Many of us prayed before and during and after abuse for deliverance, and then we waited, but we were not saved.**"**

THE DISCOVERY

When the paradigm shifts, we become open to new understanding. Insights begin to sift through the cracks in the defenses. Soon, we make a discovery that changes everything. This discovery comes with the shifting paradigm. This discovery is hard to accept, especially for someone like me, because I knew all along that I had been abused. What was I discovering? What was turning my life upside down? Wasn't this interior tumult reserved for survivors who struggled with the repressed memory?

What we discover, one way or another, is that there remains a wound, hurt, and lingering harm. That is, we face that we did not quite escape after all. I have known many survivors who did not reach this point until after retirement, but life circumstances for some of us meant we faced the past early. All of us were trying to leave the past behind, but at some point we all run into problems with our lives no longer working as we expect. We find ourselves grappling with suffering and difficulties. We start wondering why we are making choices that are not characteristic of ourselves—or at least not what we want to choose. We start wondering about certain behaviors that will not stop—or new changes in how we behave. I was well into grappling with these changes before I discovered, later, they were rooted in the abuse I mistakenly thought I had left behind me.

What is this watershed discovery? The discovery is a recognition of *the inescapable reality of abuse.* This is different from discovering things about the reality of abuse. This reckoning is with how a history of abuse affects our daily lives now—and how that history holds us back. We must realize that abuse, no matter how long ago it happened or how well buried the memories may have been, has created harm with which we must contend. It does not matter how highly functioning we are day to day, like a ghoul that haunts us and drives us to distraction, the abuse will seek to escape the darkness of its burial and be released into Light.

You could say that this discovery process coincides with the expiration date on our ability to hide the pain and agony of abuse from ourselves.

❝I would be grateful for the *bona fide* freedom, for being saved from the limitations of my own imagination.**❞**

THE PROCESS

The entire process of recovery is unpredict-able. This is good news, because our wounds hold us back from having an expansive and bold dream of healing. If we could predict the pro-cess, we would control the process. The whole point is to let go of control, to stop strangling life in an attempt to preserve our safety. We lay down our defenses and weaponry based on a leap of faith that we are safe, and that must precede the certainty that we are safe, indeed it accepts that reality that, as adults, we are never as defended as we longed to be as children who were victims.

The courage it takes to inch our way through this shift is astonishing and, in my experience, sets survivors apart from many people who have had to exercise less courage to live through a simple, normal day. For us, the change is painstakingly slow and unclear, but offers a bright ending. I understood this good news only later. At the start, I was imagining quick-fixes. I was focused on immediate problems. I had no idea what was moving up from the darkness seeking release in the Light. That is, the beginning is not only unpredictable, but it is also often unrecognizable as the beginning of anything at all. It all felt out of control and terrified me at times.

Yet the process continued like a slow-motion revelation. The ice floes howled and groaned as they broke up on a quaking river of grief. I felt the grief, but had no idea what it was. The fire of life was challenging my numbness. I felt the flood of fresh memories and emotions, but had no idea their source. The momentum was not in my control. I was told that this momentum was driven by my unconscious psyche. In the conscious world, I was impatient to figure out what was wrong in my life which had stopped working, how to fix it. That was not to be. I was terrified not to be in control of what force was upending my world. The last time I had felt that level of being out of control was when the abuse was happening. The purpose of a mastery of defenses had anticipated a lifetime of hypervigilance against the next possible attack. After all, who had ever confirmed the abuse was over? We had grown up never quite knowing. As adults we find ourselves at the end of those defenses. It is a sudden exposure that creates great distress. So, the beginning is, itself, a triggered state for many of us.

Looking back, I learned something amazing about myself. I learned that my psyche knew better than my conscious self that it was time to heal and what time it would take to heal. Our psyches are quite gentle. They are quite protective. They hold the worst of the memories and feelings for us, picking up the heaviest of the cross inflicted while we were too young to understand, and then they hold it for us until we are better able to remember and feel, accept and integrate, and survive and even flourish. Our psyches seem to me to be the greatest of all defenses, packing up all or most of the worst and holding it for us until it determines it is time to start, usually in bits and pieces, giving us back the burden so that we can be whole again. Even as our defenses are no longer working, the foundational defense, the psyche, is stepping up and taking over.

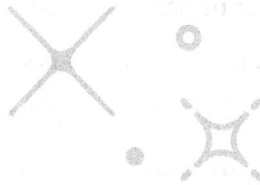

GRATITUDE

The beginning can be a source of gratitude. I look back now and am grateful that the mess of recovery started when it did, sparing me years of misery fighting to ignore memories and the effects of the abuse. In the aftermath of abuse, before we resolve many of the issues and tend many of the wounds, we engage the world with our defenses. We make choices and do things that often reflect the effects of abuse while we remain unaware. It is not a free state. These are not always free decisions. What's there to be grateful for?

The beginning made a mess of the order I had built in the aftermath of abuse, and, from the summit of that accomplishment, I resented the interruption to my life. As I discovered the lasting impact, I was angry all over again that I had been abused. I was angry that I could not leave the abuse behind me and move forward finally free. I was, at the start, angrier that the effects of abuse had persisted than that I had been abused. Why could I just not escape? Why did I find myself revisiting the past? It was like reliving the injustice. It was another round of injustice, fresh and agonizing, but it was also the completion of the injustice which I could not comprehend or fully experience as a child. I had to complete the survival, odd as that sounds. The abuse had not been fully known, and I would not have the freedom I sought until that happened.

My gratitude is a view in retrospect. I was not grateful at the beginning. My life had been upended and no longer made sense. So much I thought I had gained and built since escaping the abuse seemed lost and broken. Some of it was. The best would survive, but I had no idea. The paradigm shift underway changed everything. I was upset, angry, frustrated, and impatient, but eventually I would be grateful for the *bona fide* freedom, for being saved from the limitations of my own imagination. To be delivered from the wreckage to which I had become accustomed.

"We are like weary warriors, called to put down our armor before we can feel certain the battle is over and the war is won."

THE UNDERTOW

The shift can be a dangerous juncture because it can be interrupted by resistance we raise against it. Fortunately, our psyche releases the past slowly. It's unlikely we know that at the time. We can find ourselves running back to old defenses and coping mechanisms, like addictive or self-harming behaviors. We give in to the undertow.

What is the undertow? The undertow brings forward all the pressure we have internalized to hide the abuse. We were coerced as victims by abusers and enablers to keep the secret, to tell no one about the abuse—even to deny it to ourselves. All that coercion is so deeply ingrained in us that it is almost impossible to break the silence without personal agony. As the reality of abuse is pushing forward, the taboo of abuse is holding us back. The clash is often distressing and confusing. This is the undertow where we can lose ourselves.

Given this discomfort, it makes sense that we wish to reduce the discomfort. Especially during times when we doubt the life-changing potential of early steps in recovery. We are tempted to avoid remembering. We wonder if we might not be crazy or confused. We may identify with the abuser or enablers and think we made it up. The fact is that we might be crazy or confused.

It is good to scrutinize our memories. They come with grave accusation toward another person. It is important to wade through all the obstacles to clarity. This takes time. Doubt can be a very helpful ingredient in remaining restless until we get to the bedrock of reality. Most survivors I know subject their remembering process to relentless scrutiny.

No one needs certainty more than survivors,

because we will build our future wellness on our ability to believe our memories. To get there, we need time, and a safe setting, and compassionate and knowledgeable help in order to sort through the shards of memories at the excavation site. We need to rediscover and accept the darker elements of memories which we thought were benign.

This is why it is good to find professional help to walk through these early steps. It is also good to find experienced peers who can affirm the process. It is good to have someone to support us in different ways we address the wounds of the past. In other words, it is good to have or develop a network of safe support.

What many of us do, instead, is resist. It can be preferable to be crazy or grossly mistaken than to accept the full brunt of abuse. (For a long time, I thought it was.) We are motivated to doubt. We give doubt too much credence. We reject hints of darkness starting to appear

in once-benign memories. We resist the new
memories that vie for our attention. We reject
old feelings that interrupt daily life. Instead of
moving forward with a process of discovery, we
judge feelings. We dismiss memories. We create
an undertow that threatens our recovery by rejecting and judging and doubting that we were
abused. The fact is that we can remain flailing
in resistance for a very long time.

Yet who can blame us for not wanting this to
be true? Who would volunteer to revisit horror
in a past we thought was left behind us? Walking
back into the past through the melee of memories and feelings is the stuff of a horror-movie
plot. We resist because we think we are protecting people and relationships, however precarious
they may be. We resist to maintain the illusion
that we control our lives, having known how
out-of-control life can be in abuse. We might
fight to preserve our defenses as the memory of
abuse emerges. The fact of recovery is that the

feelings get worse before they get better, and we can end up floundering in the undertow that prefers the known suffering to the hints of new life.

These are some reasons why the most courageous steps which a survivor will ever take are the first steps in the beginning of recovery. These are often very private and lonely steps. After we start, there is a certain momentum. Before we start, we face disorientation, loss, with the only gain (it can seem) in more pain and suffering. In the absence of helpers, there may seem no clear promise about the outcome.

" There was a divine spark within me which abuse could not extinguish, and which came back from dark embers to full flame, drawing life from what is divine far beyond me. **"**

WHY ME?

Many of us prayed before and during and after abuse for deliverance, and then we waited, but we were not saved. The Almighty must have had reasons not to intervene. I'm not worth saving, or so the child concludes.

Not chosen by God for rescue, we were indeed chosen by our abusers, with dire consequences. God created us human. The experience of abuse is dehumanizing. That can be more than a feeling. It can become an identity.

To achieve their own ends, abusers and their enablers confuse what victims meekly know. Insisting we want to be abused, they isolate us in their deceit, and we have no alternative to their authority. It can seem like no one else considers this a crisis. Maybe it doesn't matter.

Here begin the shame, confusion, fright, self-recrimination, anger, grief, distrust and other aspects of the heavy burden we will shoulder into adulthood. As their impact accumulates, we may feel worse. Sometimes we believe we are uniquely undeserving after all, making it more not less difficult to refute abusers and their enablers.

Compared to this psychological rip tide, religion can feel shallow and, given the Church's response in my early life, ineffective. Yet, I kept encountering remarkable people who believed in something stronger than the evil that had secretly triumphed in my life. It was impossible (though I did try) to reject their claim that we are called by name and saved at a great price. Perhaps I might not be worthless after all. Such was the great gift of psychic dissonance which would anchor me in Jesus Christ.

Asking Why Me? Turned out to be an exercise in understanding my own place in the world. It opened me to asking about my true value and purpose, and with the remnants of the faith that had been bruised in the Church I found, as I kept wondering, something of what it means to be chosen by God not for suffering but for new life.

"We are brought to a psychological excavation site, where we slowly, perhaps begrudgingly, begin to see something that lies buried in darkness which must be brought into the Light.**"**

WHY, GOD?

Adult life may become safe enough to rage at God for failing to stop the abuse. Or, life may reflect the tumult of childhood, leaving our feelings buried alongside our unfinished business with God. In time we may forgive people who failed to protect us, but resentment toward God can still simmer. After all, most adults will ac- knowledge other adults fall short, but God? Perfection has no excuse for failure.

Age compounded my complaint toward God. I met more and more people who, worthy unlike myself, still suffered unjustly and terribly. Why, God?

The Church had lost credibility by abandoning tens of thousands of child victims for decades. Religious people, psychologists, legislators and attorneys had participated in ignoring or blaming and silencing us en masse. These were the holy, the ordained, the credentialed, and the educated elite. They were the pillars of society. Why, God, why? My therapist listened with compassion, but, in the end, as with all good therapy, she had no answers for me. I was left to find an answer, and I was struggling not just with God's non-response but also with a cruel Church. My therapist had her own understandable anger at the Church on my behalf. It added to an internal resistance to any breakthrough in hearing God's meaning in God's deafening silence.

While helpful, therapy fell short. Its medical model defined what I had experienced as pathology, but I knew it was evil. In the ascendancy of evil, only faith—with or without the Church— would do.

In faith, there is a truth no abuser can pervert. No stupidity among the powerful can harm it. Professionals and experts and scholars cannot revise it to protect their artful rationalizations. It cannot be twisted by enablers and sympathizers. Here is that from which evil recoils. It was only here where I could rebuild my life safely, starting by unearthing my buried grief and unresolved questions.

"We need to rethink and
re-feel and rebuild.**"**

MIRROR

We are most often people of shame. We hide the truth of ourselves, almost all of ourselves, in particular that we survived being victims of abuse. We can feel today as ugly as the abuse made us feel decades earlier. We emerge from a childhood of abuse into an adult world where we, at least in part, hide behind false personas or dangerous chemicals or compulsive behaviors, or we hide in isolation. Our disguises are artful as our hearts ache for loving kindness.

Now and then, we venture to share our story with someone who seems to be compassionate or wise, people most often are silenced, or look away, or avoid us out of their own sense of lack or horror. Or, they react and tell us to "get over it" as if we can flip a switch on our healing. Or, they try to meddle and fix us with advice, mostly to relieve their own anxiety encountering such pain or evil. Or, they invite us to pick up the fight to confront the broken system, before we have even mastered the shocking difficulty in making good, healthful choices in our wounded lives. Such reactions can reinforce our sense of shame, our experience of pain, and our need to hide.

In media, where abuse victims at least are not ignored, we see images of ourselves mostly as pathetic or devious people driven to violence or dissolution. The message is that victimhood is destiny and despair. To preserve how people see us, we work doubly to avoid being associated with these caricatures. There seems to be no image of hope for us.

Along the *Via Dolorosa*, Jesus was dragging his Cross—and our redemption—on the torn flesh of his abused and wounded body. Veronica slipped out of the crowd to wipe His face with a moist cloth. The image He gave her was formed in blood and dirt and sweat. She beheld that image with her broken heart and saw beauty.

"Memories like magma were forcing a pathway upward to release, shimmying through layers of sediment and resistance, creating quakes and shudders, sending forward inexplicable geysers of emotions.**"**

SAFETY

Sometimes we have picked up where the abuser left off destroying our very person. We self- harm to continue the destruction and pain of our bodies. We are drawn to attempt suicide to complete the murder of self the predator began. Or, we abuse substances, or replace the abuser with dangerous people and situations in our adult lives. As the life-and-death crisis continues, healing begins with sometimes no more than a longing or desire to escape.

One helpful tool in adding safety to our recovery is some advance work. We can make a phone list of people who are safe to call when we need help. Different people are right for different needs. The number we call for help when we are confused is very different from the one we call if we become suicidal. Having all our numbers listed and available in several places is a smart safety measure.

Knowing who to call for what kind of help is about roles. Roles are about expectations. With a damaging figure dominating our early lives and eclipsing others' roles protecting us, sorting through roles and expectations can get confusing. So, making out a phone list is a great exercise in understanding the different roles different people play as unique pieces of a quilt we are stitching together a little at a time.

It also helps us grapple with how everyone to whom we turn will be limited, because everyone is human. The exception is God, Who is the only sure footing for our long-term recovery.

LIES

It was like a shroud, how lies were wrapped around the truth of our suffering—for years, sometimes forever. The predator was more powerful and more credible. Some of us even tried to tell our truth while the abuse was going on, but we were not believed. We have been called the liars, while we watched a world full of enablers support the liars as they flourished. Words have been perverted, except for one Word. He is Truth, and He is the first word in which some of us can gain new trust. There were parents and teachers and other adults who, for whatever reason, did not protect us. Their authority was not true in the presence of the evil of abuse. There was the Church hierarchy, which silenced our truth or denounced us, or whose attorneys attacked us as liars. There were lay Catholics who dismissed us as litigious or pitied us as if we were hopeless. Yet, there we were, with a truth burning in our hearts to be revealed so it could be healed. We knew better than those who failed us that we cannot heal ourselves. Though our stories are very different, we, too, have the same need for a Savior.

Over the years, it has become so apparent to me how little the expert class and hierarchy understand the nature of abuse for its lies. So many people mistake the nature of abuse in that way, and in that I see the impact of abuse which I suffered continuing to this day, beyond my psyche and into the full Church and society which still grapple with its simple unequivocal evil.

CHOICE

Choice is the first thing a predator destroys. Before the abuse actually begins, grooming methodically blurs judgment for a child and for his or her caretakers. Before the first recovery book is opened or the first therapist office is dialed, there is a choice inside. It's often a ferocious "No!" to an entire lifestyle or relationship or compulsion. It has to be strong enough to counter all the ingrained resistance inside one s heart and in the company of family, friends, and society. This is for many a true life-and-death choice to choose not to be a victim any longer.

Emerging from a victims life to a survivor attitude can be daunting. It's very clear we have to learn new rules for living in some or all areas of our lives. After we learn them, we must choose them, sometimes again and again and again. Rejecting the past becomes an immediate matter—as we consciously begin to make daily choices for life and not for more of the death of abuse. That is the very freedom of choice the abuser destroyed; we are grown now, and able to choose against the brutality. We can choose to seek a new life.

After exile, God does bring His people back to a safe place and a new life to flourish in the good, right order He is restoring. And he gives us a choice, "I have set before you life and death, the blessing and the curse. Choose life."[1]

1. Deuteronomy 30:19

PRICE

For most of us, there's a price to choosing healing, and even a price to returning to the Church in any way—even exploratory ways. Scars of abuse on family systems and friendships respond, like any scar, inflexibly, even rigidly. To seek help is to expose the secret. To seek help is to acknowledge one or more abusers along with people who enabled them. Some abusers made victims of all family members, but some were explicitly enabled by another adult as well.

To seek help is to threaten the system of relationships built on hiding the real workings, and indeed can challenge a family to confront the fact that an abuser (e.g., grandfather, priest, uncle) is still roaming freely at family functions with access to children. In the case of the undetected priest abuser, we have faced their presence at family gatherings, funerals, and weddings. The sicker the system, the higher the price will be exacted from the victim who dares to seek healing, which requires truth to long for and truth to proceed.

Too many survivors will walk into therapy for the first time or into spiritual direction having been denounced or persecuted by their own families for this brave step. Our first step can feel dangerous because it is. While we are no longer children in the hands of abusers, we may be taking steps to upend our world of relationships as we know them—and to surrender what is familiar and comfortable (even if it is no longer working).

I know of another price, the price survivors of clergy abuse have been to find some safe connection with the faith they love in connection with an errant Church. It is a price little noticed, indeed underestimated. Sometimes, people assume no price is paid and that survivors leave the Church (or should leave the Church). Other times, as with abuse itself, people cannot comprehend. For example, I know survivors whose allegations against abusers were dismissed, with abusers remaining active and unsanctioned in the Church, while the survivor still found a way or place to be safe within the institution to be close to the sacraments. For them, every time stepping into a Church building for Mass is a crucible which, I know, is wedded to Christ on His Cross, but from what hands have those particular stripes been struck?

"The beginning coincides with the expiration date stamped on our ability to hide the pain and the agony of abuse from ourselves.**"**

THE RIPPLE EFFECT

To understand other issues that may be obstacles to healing from abuse it's worth considering the ripple effort of abuse.

Abuse is a terrible wound inflicted on a victim, but its impact does not end with us. Abuse has a disastrous ripple effect expanding outward from us in the lives of all the people who connect to us. They have lost, along with us, all that we might have been in their lives.

Assuming a parent is not the abuser, abuse by another ruptures the bond of trust in protection and care a child has for a parent. This rupture needs healing, and healing through reconciliation can be possible. Where abuse remains secret, as it most often does, that rupture colors a primary relationship for the child, and for the parents from whom their child is to some degree alienated. That wounded relationship and those dire losses do not heal of their own accord. The free flow of love is reduced or ended.

Assuming a sibling is not the abuser, abuse by another person disrupts the bond of confidence and the opportunities for being known freely by a loved age-mate or equal. These sibling losses and wounds are family losses and wounds, because where signs of rupture—anger, resentment, withdrawal—affect one sibling relationship, they also affect all other relationships which must accommodate them.

These illustrate just a few ways that the effects of abuse ripple out from the prime suffering target of abuse, affecting relationships from close family members, through extended family, friends, schools, parishes, communities. And that is during the era when our original family is intact and when abuse has relatively recently happened.

The terrible impact of abuse ripples outward over time. Its harm is not limited to relationships that exist at the time of abuse. Studies show what survivors have been recounting to the listening Church for decades. Our spouses and children bear the wounds of abuse in different ways. A wife may never know her husband fully until years after the wedding he shifts from a functioning if guarded man to a man who has stopped functioning when memories hit. Children often sense and even act out their abused parent's emotional state, showing inclinations to mental illness and suicidality as if on the parent's behalf. Then there is the drama in the original family—among parents, siblings, extended family, and friends—when abuse is revealed; once relatively unified families are known to break into camps based on reactions to the survivor's revelation, or to unify in rejecting the survivor who reveals the taboo, or to rally behind a survivor and against the perpetrator. In any event, a family status is utterly changed years after the abuse. And what about the friends and colleagues who do not have full access to a wonderful person who remains wounded by unresolved abuse issues?

Even as we are staggered by the reality of this devastation, there is hope. First, there is hope in all suffering. This is why my faith was critical in my own recovery. Abuse is suffering. Healing hurts because it revisits suffering; so, healing is suffering. What is the point of anything but denial? It becomes existential. All people suffer, and part of living is grappling with the mystery of suffering—whether life is even worth it given the price exacted. Victims of abuse suffer in particular ways, so we grapple with the mystery of suffering in a particular way. Therapy can explore that and challenge a person to find meaning in suffering, but only Christ died to give suffering redemptive meaning.

That is why there is hope in all suffering. One way we see hope in the suffering of abuse is to look at the ripple effect of suffering caused when a single child is abused. Look closely at the moment when the pebble first hits the water to start all the reaction. That is the dark encounter. Picture, now, how a different encounter can have the opposite effect. The survivor who heals sends similar ripples; I have witnessed that repeatedly in my work. The family member who, even if alone without any other person supporting him or her, seeks truth and understanding and receives healing; others will benefit from this healing, too. I have witnessed, too, parishioners who turn around the devastation of hearing about abuse in their midst and create a safe and loving environment for the survivor, his or her family—and by extension all survivors and all families.

Don't despair. The ripple effect works both ways—for harm and for healing. Which is why I do the work I do. It is an act of hope from the strike point of abuse in a way that only a victim,

an abuser, or the priest whom the abuser imper-
sonated can provide.

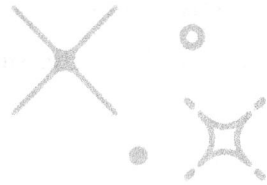

FAITH'S ROLE

Many people struggle to understand why faith is considered a unique element in healing. This is related, I suspect, to people thinking that the spirituality, which is routinely part of the discussion in mainstream therapy, suffices in healing. For many people, it does. For those who need more, there is seldom more available. That is why I do the work I do.

Ironically, many Catholics, in being defensive when it comes to the abuse scandals within the Church, undervalue the role of faith in hope for healing from abuse. To refute the onslaught of lawsuits which have been significantly (although not solely) focused on the Catholic Church for many years, Catholics point out that abuse happens everywhere, and they are right. However, to minimize the particularly egregious wound of abuse within the Church—especially by clergy—is to dismiss the power of faith, indeed, to contribute to the idea of priests as something inconsequential. While it is true that the wound of abuse by a parent or a sibling or a coach will have signature effects, no matter how much is lost in these horrific experiences the Church always remains a place of last refuge. Where there is no other safety, the historical idea of sanctuary meant something. Sanctuary was denied no one. For the victim of clergy abuse, however, not only do family and all other relationships suffer devastating harm, but also there is no other safety. There is no concept of sanctuary.

It is true that the world beyond the Church focuses special attention on abuse within the Church while incidents of abusers outside the Church are far more frequent. It is true that there are those who capitalize on that intense emotion for their own ends, such as driving clicks to a website or dollars to a coffer. Yet, these groups would not have the opportunity if there were no abuse. The existence of trends of abuse within the Church is the first problem. All else flows from that, including many other injustices and wrongs.

The Church still, after all these years, evokes public reaction stronger than abuse in other settings. This is a testimony truer than that of Catholics insisting there should be no distinctions made—or that, based on lower incidence, there is a lesser problem. Why are the defenders wrong and the critics right?

Because of the facts of abuse. Trust was breached all those years ago, and the rupture remains, as it remains in any family. There is a rupture where somewhere in the social psyche the idea of sanctuary was secure, until the sanctuary was destroyed. Society in decrying the abuse is crying for the sanctuary. We, in the

Church, in denying the depth of loss felt in society, remain deaf.

There is another reason faith is critical. It is one of the primary reasons I came back to the faith after rejecting it in the wake of my first-person experience of systemic institutional abuse. In the end, for me, as effective as therapy was, it fell short explaining abuse. In its medical model, abuse was a pathology. It was one of the worst pathologies, and at the time there was almost universal agreement that child sexual abuse was wrong, But even then, the science of psychology had no way to name or deal with evil. What I had experienced was evil, perhaps also pathology, but evil. I have written about that in other places, but for now what matters is that, for me and many other survivors of abuse, until we can grapple with the depth of the evil perpetrated upon us, we cannot fully make peace with the past. In that sense, faith was more than a way to comfort and soothe myself, as my then-therapist viewed it. It was the only way to deal with the fundamental reality of what evil had happened to me in the house of the Lord.

" No one needs certainty about what we remember more than survivors, because we know we are about to rebuild our future on what we learn about our past. **"**

HALF REALITIES

I participate in panels which include medical or professionally trained people who are explaining to audiences aspects of the scandal of abuse in the Church. Inevitably, I sit through one expert or other projecting the "doomsday slide." This slide has a list of all the ways abuse leaves us damaged human beings worthy of pity; e.g., addictions, mental illness, divorce, failures. There has never been, in my 20 years of experience, a slide that describes the remarkable attributes of survivors of abuse—except for my presentation. I usually begin by asking the prior speaker to return to his or her "doomsday slide" so I can add other ways we bear unbearable crosses, and then I show my slide of all the gifts which survivors whom I have known bring to relationships; e.g., courage, resilience, the kindness learned only in suffering, distrust of authority, tenacity.

Why do people offer pity instead of compassion? Pity keeps the terrifying reality of abuse at arm's length. It is something that happens to the other.

We can't blame the person who hides behind pity, even though it can hurt to feel ourselves put at arm's length because of cruelty we did not commit. I understand. Yet we need to carefully select those to whom we turn. For our own sakes we have to be realistic. For many good people it is simply too difficult to be forced to see, in stories we tell seeking kindness, the darkness and depravity of humanity in full display. Still other people are struggling in private hell, and hearing about abuse can be too close for now or possibly forever. I understand—and encourage fellow survivors to understand—that some family and friends may seem like the logical first option for confidantes, but that certain levels of detail and intense emotional processing are often best done with professionals, although that is not a hard and fast rule. This preserves time with family and friends for special and loving encounters which can be supportive but not burdened with the role which a trained professional best can handle. This helps, too, give family and friends time to process their own intense emotions about our suffering. They may want to speak with a therapist as well. Not asking people close to us to make up for all the need the wound of abuse has inflicted is a very wonderful way to get all the best from family and friends who want to support us.

There is no doubt that we who have suffered abuse bear deep wounds. The good news is that we can recover. The "doomsday slide" is not our destiny. It lists only symptoms, and only reflects half of the reality of who we are.

Wherever we find our experience only half represented, it's good to understand a few things.

The world often recoils from abuse for its horror, but in faith we have the ability to look at any suffering and, without denying or minimizing its horror, have the Perfect Victim showing us the hope and the new life to which it can lead. This life is not the same as it would have been had we not been abused. Our Savior rose from the dead restoring our Eternal Life, but His hands, feet, and side still bore the wounds.

There is no doubt that abuse within the Church inflicts an additional dimension of loss and agony on us, and on others. This, too, is only half the story. The other half of the story is that we have survived, that we can become wise and strong and loving in ways that only suffering can forge in a heart. In healing, we will come to see the full reality of our having survived abuse— and can we see our beauty.

FIRST PRINCIPLE

Having considered these ideas so far, now it is possible to consider the first principle in serving to help survivors of abuse—or anyone really—heal from abuse, from its damage, from how it contorts responses, from how it damages the body, from how it tangles up emotional skills needed for relationships. The first principle is that each survivor is God's remarkable creation and, when God finished His Creation with the man and the woman before Him, He saw that it was good. And God was pleased.[2]

Each creation is unique and a delight to God. We are the apple of His eye.[3] No one

---

2. Genesis 1:31. "God looked at everything he had made, and found it very good. Evening came, and morning followed—the sixth day.
3. Deuteronomy 32:10. "He found them in a wilderness, a wasteland of howling desert. He shielded them, cared for them, guarded them as the apple of his eye."

of us is the same. That is why not one of our experiences of abuse—even if the instance of abuse were exactly replicated factors, including same age, same place, same abuser—is the same. Abuse, like grace, works on nature—showing abuse to be evil, and even of that which some call antichrist.

Distinctions do not alienate us from each other's experiences. For example, common effects of abuse are known. Commonalities are important, even if looking at the negative impact we see just half the story. Seeing that story is important.

Commonalities also help break the isolation and shame that comes while we are at that point when we believe we are the only ones, we are a "freak of nature," we should hide our faces. Learning we are not the only ones who suffer is a remarkable freedom. Comparing ways in which we experience the effects of abuse and learn to overcome the wounds is a rich experience. We can affirm each other's progress because we know the common struggle.

We often turn to therapy, which makes great use of commonalities to shed light on the experience of abuse and the process of healing. Here is a common language. We use it to stand on the shoulders of giants as we draw on centuries of thought and literature to find our own path to a new life. The language of the experts and the researchers, however, has traditionally been that of diagnosis, indeed illness. The danger comes when diagnostic commonalities become mistaken for wisdom in pastoral care or in friendships. There is great value in the therapeutic pursuit, except when it is mistaken for the whole solution. A diagnosis is not an identity.

Each survivor leaves a distinct image on the veil raised to comfort us and offer relief. To the person who responds to our suffering with good intention, do not compound injustice already done by treating us like a single, simplistic caricature. This is de-personalizing. It is de-humanizing. To hold this image up for us to see, solely, as our identity is to mistake a single facet for the whole. It is, as I sometimes say, the little-known sin of synecdoche.

Look at abuse in all its dimensions if you want to find the full, rich treasury of dimension of the person whom God created, an abuser harmed, and the one true Savior can lead to new life. Do not impose your expectations on what healing should look like. Do not bring judgment to how victims survive. It is enough for a prayerful Christian to turn his or her eyes on our suffering to see our resilience and to support our triumph. This is the image of hope in suffering, where it is not required to deny or diminish suffering. Serving this image, you are serving the many faces of God.

THE SECOND WOUND

To help anyone along their early steps in recovery, it is important to understand how the wound of abuse or trauma can compound over time.

There is the first or primary wound of abuse, but there are many, many other wounds that compound the impact of abuse. In a way abuse is death by a million cuts—cuts to body, mind, heart, and spirit. These are all the secondary wounds.

Nowhere are we more re-wounded than at that time we dare to step forward to trust someone—after years of silence—with our story to seek help and solace. There are many ways an adult survivor may be wounded at this point again—by a dismissive family member, by an argumentative parishioner, by an aggressive attorney representing the Church. I'm not suggesting other people not have their own reactions, but I'm suggesting it's worth knowing the full impact of how any person decides to react to an allegation of abuse.

There is quite a bit of risk involved when a survivor ventures forward to share some portion of a story of suffering. It is a juncture when we are most often re-wounded, usually due to ignorance, sometimes due to resistance. Someone says the wrong thing. Worse, someone is insensitive or cruel. This re-wounding is a strike on the still-pained wound of abuse, and it can be reason why a survivor withdraws and declines to seek compassion from others.

The wound of abuse can rupture our ability to trust in all authority that failed us. It certainly can mix us up about authority. That includes the greatest authority, God. In that sense, every story of abuse is a faith story. Every story of abuse is every story in Scripture. As for that risk of re-wounding? It includes a risk of wounding an already-wounded faith. It includes a risk of harming, sometime permanently, someone's ability to dare to find new and better relationships. Faith stories are as unique as every child of God. This is true as well for the faith stories of every survivor of abuse. It is in telling our faith stories that we integrate our Catholic faith into a broader recovery process which includes able professional care. To tell the story, we need time to follow the threads of faith through the scar— or the blood—and that is why when someone ventures forward they are terribly vulnerable. They are close to the original pain of betrayal and harm. The lifelong defenses are down. The re-wounding at this point reaches unencumbered that far back.

For survivors, working through our story with an awareness of that spiritual dimension of us who is drawn to long for God is, in my view, central to healing. This is different from how, for example, survivors of abuse within the Catholic Church relate to the institutional Church and her sacramental life. To hear the reality in the faith story with which you may be entrusted is to understand this distinction. I recall one deacon who aspired to work with survivors of abuse, but he insisted that they could not be healed if they did not learn to agree with his political view of Church liturgical reforms. I knew the survivors he met would likely be struggling at a far more fundamental level of faith. He was both blinded to their reality by his own need for a triumphant point of view, and he was a high risk when encountering a survivor who might reach out for care who happened, at that moment in time, to disagree with his truth.

Ultimately, survivors of abuse within the Church may be psychologically or emotionally safe at a distance from the Church practices, or not at all. It may be possible only after a long time to explore a relationship with the Church. One way to undermine a survivor's chances of finding some peace with the Church is by judging as the deacon may have—that is, by wounding with judgment.

There is a treasure to be found exploring the faith experience in our stories even when we have rejected the Catholic faith or Church entirely. We can still explore the critical distinction between true faith and the perversion of faith by abusers. Making these distinctions may help you find peace with the faith so that you are free you to deepen your relationship with God in other, safer settings.

"Everyone to whom we turn will be limited, because everyone is human. The exception is God.**"**

FIRST MEMORIES

I have had the privilege of being a pastoral companion for survivors of abuse as they grapple with the kinds of disturbances that involve the appearances of bits and pieces of memories that force a person to recognize he or she was abused in some way. The first and most hard-and-fast rule is to stay far back from the action, where the confusion and upset are roiling, and not influence what is happening in this person's life, aside from ensuring they are safe and have all the support they need.

Survivors have a lonely road ahead. No one can go into this process with us. No one can carry this Cross for us. We can lean on people. There will be the Simons of Cyrene. But anyone who seeks to support a survivor in this early process needs to honor that separateness and independence, first, and then find ways to listen, care, and support without becoming involved or even influential. Becoming enmeshed in the process undermines the survivor and hints at a confusion who the process is supposed to benefit—the survivor with a painful healing, or you with the temporary relief you can feel by getting too involved.

There are a couple things that may be helpful, however, to state about the remembering process. First, remembering is a process that varies widely. Some people remember completely, although they may not grapple with the impact until later years. Their memories may be fully intact but "suppressed," in that, for a broad-stroke idea, they are divorced from feelings which are often still rattling around inside the survivor unhealed. Often, however, memories appear or are clarified early in this process.

Memories finish differently from how they start. They do not come to us wrapped up, making sense, connected to the senses and emotions we experienced during them, all in a single piece. They come to us as a mess most often, and disconnected from sensations and feelings that need to be reconnected. They may never be fully recovered yet can be reliable for what they are needed to do in our lives.

Memories are not necessarily chronological, and they can be highly subjective or interpretive. So, what a survivor is recounting early in the process may need time and healing to become really clear. That does not mean the early memory is false, but that the remembering process is just that, a process. Only by looking at what the psyche delivers up out of the depths can we begin to see a full memory in time.

Memories are not always visual. I'd go so far as to say memories are often emotional or sensations, with the visual following second. So, if a survivor is feeling overwhelmed, we may not need to wait for that memory causing the feeling to pop up. Being overwhelmed may be the memory. What more natural feeling to have to remember at all from being abused, than to be overwhelmed? The same would be true for rage, disgust, fright, hurt, abandonment ... to name a few.

The most important thing about receiving memories from our past is to receive without judgment. The most important thing about receiving the gift of a survivor sharing their memory is to receive without judgment. The need to have a memory pristine and clear enough for a court of law falls into a very narrow slice of life—that is, in reporting. The greater portion of remembering is about the messy process of sorting through and understanding in small steps. To rush that or press that process is to undermine its efficacy.

LIMITED EXPERTISE

Early steps into recovery involve a sudden experience of overwhelming need. It can feel huge, and it can send us running like people escaping a fire where there is not enough water. In that time, it is not uncommon to seek the one person with the right answer that works as the key needed to unlock the gate and free us from the flames. In short order, we learn that is not how it works.

No one is fully qualified to help a survivor of abuse heal. We will need many people over time helping us in different ways. That does not happen right away, and that is a good thing. We need to take our time to sort through what we need and who can help us.

As we walk through the remembering and healing process, we start to see that there is not one all-consuming need but rather different needs for different times. In abuse, we often learned to hide our needs. Or being neglected did not learn we had needs and what to do about them. Recovery will start looking at those individually. The great undifferentiated whole will start becoming manageable small pieces. In the process, we can set aside the desperate search for the one person, the one savior, the one answer. We can shift into relying on a network of support. That network consists of different types of gifts and talents and training and personalities. We piece together a whole that is varied. It has something for all our different needs.

Building that network takes time, and it takes a lot of courage. Every person who ends up within this sacred circle involves a whole process of approach, trust, sharing—and sorting through who knows what, who is there for what....

Meanwhile, we need to grieve that a common wish to be saved isn't something any person can deliver. The resolution will not be that simple. There will be no catalytic answer. This is a path to be walked, not a click to conclusion. There may be one person who is a primary inspiration or helper. There may be a few people who become the ones who help us turn the corners we would not have turned without them.

Yet even the most devoted spouse, who is selflessly intent on helping us heal, cannot truly deliver us from the suffering of abuse. For that, there is one Savior, and for many people wounded within the Church that relationship has been wounded along with all other relationships. The healing supported by the network of trusted people provides relationships which, one hopes, can offer better experiences and growing confidence that trusting and loving others does not lead to harm. Ultimately, as our ability to be in relationships becomes more confident, we find our relationship with God—notice I did not say with the Church—improve.

It takes time to create this network of diversified support. Often, I am blessed to know a survivor at the beginning of their process of healing. They have no network, yet. They often have no therapist or have left a therapist. It is very common that they have had no connection with faith, either. So, we start at the beginning. I have a list of referrals for therapists. I know what to do if someone is in a crisis that requires medical care. I know about shelters, centers, and 12 Step programs, and other resources. One of the most important things to know is that there are resources for solving most problems. One of the most important things to have is a list of reputable resources and the time to help a survivor take the first steps to find a surround of support.

There are two ways to be sure that, in offering care to survivors in these early steps toward healing, you do not succumb to the temptation to play a greater role than your limited expertise

warrants. One is to develop your own list of resources and referrals. The other is to remember
that you are not the savior. You will not heal
any one of us. Your role is guide and possibly
spiritual midwife, but always remember that,
even as we seek intensely in the early recovery
process for the answer, for the solution, for the
cure, for the savior who can make it all go away,
there is only one Savior who will ask each of
us to walk through the process, accept the *Via
Dolorosa*, and find a new life. He alone has that
qualification because He alone already walked
that way.

"Words have been
perverted, except for one
Word. That Word is Truth, and
He is the first word on which
any of us can rely entirely
with spontaneous joy.**"**

SHAME

We survivors are often people of shame. We hide the truth of ourselves, almost all of ourselves, in particular the truth that we survived being victims of abuse. The less we have dealt with the abuse of the past the more likely we can feel today as ugly as the abuse made us feel then. We emerge from a childhood of abuse into an adult world where we, at least in part, hide behind false personas or dangerous chemicals or compulsive behaviors, or we hide in isolation. Our disguises are artful as our hearts ache for loving kindness.

We may venture to share our story with someone who seems to be compassionate or wise. It took all our courage, yet their immediate reaction falls short of what we needed. Even the most competent or compassionate people, caught unawares, most often are silenced, or look away, or avoid us out of their own sense of lack or horror when first faced with the fact that we have suffered. We've lived with this story all our lives. There is nothing shocking to us, but we will face the shock of others. It's a good idea not to interpret their first reaction as what to expect. People need time sometimes. It's good to give them time—as well as to choose carefully who we tell first.

The fact is that sometimes we tell the wrong people first. We can survive the hurt, but it is its own wound. It is a second wound that inflames our shame when people minimize our suffering and tell us to' "get over it" (as if we can flip a switch on our healing). Or they try to meddle and fix us with advice; we can feel their anxiety and need to relieve their own distress by making our pain stop. Or they invite us to pick up the fight to confront a broken system, which no one will deny is broken, before we have mastered the shocking difficulty in making good, healthful choices in our wounded lives. Such reactions can reinforce our sense of shame, our experience of pain, our doubt in our own instincts, and our need to hide. Such reactions deliver a second wound. It's important to know many of us had to endure this kind of wounding but still found good, healthy support from others.

It's important to seek, tirelessly and with grief, if need be, sources of the true image of ourselves. If someone proves unable to support us, move on. Don't stay and argue lest you lose your focus on your need to heal, and the need to heal is of primary importance. On your healing resides all the hope for a new and better future. One element in a healthy recovery is that we keep moving. Keep looking for the things that help and keep discarding things that do not. We do not need to end relationships that do not help, but we can set them aside for a while.

We do not need to react places or situations permanently, but we do need to limit ourselves to what helps recovery move forward. In the early phase of recovery, our main goal is as if we are taking a journey and need to sort through what will help us along the way. The journey is our personal *Via Dolorosa*.

There is also something else about our shame to know, even if it takes a long time to absorb into our consciousness. I learned it when I was balking against the idea that my therapist suggested. To offset my low self-esteem, she wanted me to speak affirmations aloud to myself; for example, I am a good person. Yet why would I believe myself if I had so little esteem for what I had to say? What helped me was to realize that my opinion—however low or high—I had of myself was none of my business. What people thought of me was none of my business. What mattered was God's view of me, and for that I kept reading Scripture that spoke about a relentless love for me that would stop at nothing to bring me to Him safely and fulfilled, not abused and wounded.

"Friendships in Christ offer remarkable healing for all survivors of any abuse, but especially for those abused within the Church.**"**

SELF-CARE

We survivors are responsible for our own safety. In our first steps toward recovery from abuse or trauma, it can be incomprehensible to seek help, but if there is an emergency we must. One reason some of us move toward recovery is because someone we love is pushing us in that direction, despite our resistance. Seeking recovery is itself a step toward safety, too.

It's one thing to share our stories with someone for the first time. That is a risk and requires courage—and a willingness to walk away if the person does not respond well. We also need to reflect on something about our safety that is important when we begin to share our stories.

So often the story we tell can be entirely told in past tense. Yet we are living in a current situation. We are in a current emotional state. One of the most important questions to ask ourselves when we dare to share our stories is: Am I safe right now? If the answer is "no," it is important to share your fear with the person you've turned to. Let them help you.

Sometimes we have picked up where the abuser left off destroying our very person. We self-harm to continue the destruction and pain of our bodies. We are drawn to attempt suicide to complete the murder of self the predator began. Or we abuse substances. Or we replace the abuser with dangerous people and situations in our adult lives. Or we marry or are in a relationship with a new abuser.

As survivors we need to know resources available to help us. Yet when we are moving into recovery for the first time, we may be too stressed to do research that otherwise would be easy for us. There are many help lines. (Many are listed as Hotlines on SpiritFire.Online.) Also, make a phone list of people who are safe to call when we need help. When we are in crisis, we can forget there are even people there to call! At one point, I shared my list with all its members, so they knew they could reach out to each other if they needed help in supporting me.

"Our disguises are as
artful as our hearts ache
for loving kindness.**"**

WOUNDED HEALER

Looking forward into a future that is freed from the burden of abuse, it is enough for us to imagine living lives that are purposeful, contented, and free. It can be a heavy burden to expect that we all become "wounded healers." Many people use this idea as just another way to short circuit the long process of recovery. There is no shortcut. The whole precious value of the wounded healer is having walked the difficult path others have not, having returned intact and healed, and only then being able to help others find the way.

Carl Jung wrote about how the best psychotherapists are themselves wounded and well familiar with their shadow self. He used the term "wounded healer" before Henri Nouwen spoke about the need for Christian ministry that spoke from first-person wounds. He wrote about the best guide to find a way through the desert is one who has been there and knows the way. He talked about putting our wounds in the service of others, assuming we had experienced healing ourselves in Christ. This is one of the reasons I have been inspired to do what I do.

There is no doubt in my mind, from my years of pastoral work in this area, that survivors who heal bring healing to their families, friends, the Church, and the world. Often that is unconscious. Being well brings wellness options elsewhere. Being healed is an antidote to the ruptures in relationships caused by unresolved pain.

Additionally, some of us find ways to put our suffering in the service of others. It starts with stories that have integrated faith in an authentic and unique way into a trauma experience that is unique as well. It becomes a testimony of glory to God. Only when a survivor is ready to give away their story—and there is more loss and grief than may seem obvious in doing so—that they can become a peer guide for others in pastoral ministries within the Church. This is no academic exercise, and it is not something a degree of study can secure.

"The beginning is not only unpredictable, but it is also often unrecognizable as the beginning of anything at all— just chaos and discomfort."

DIMENSIONS OF HEALING

There are many dimensions to the human person, and in most cases every dimension of a person is harmed in some way by abuse. That is how far abuse strikes at each of us, especially a child or vulnerable person who have less capacity to process and compartmentalize in a healthy way. There are very real effects of abuse physically, some that last a lifetime and need care. Many types of medicine address lasting impact, although many physicians are not sensitive to the issues related to abuse. Often alternative medicine has practitioners more attuned to issues of abuse, and the effects of cortisol-overload, but not all offer research-based care or have the same stringent ethical codes of mainstream health care.

Therapy addresses the psychological and emotional wounds and can sometimes have a positive effect on relationships. Some types of therapy focus largely on the social or relational effects of abuse—as well as, more recently, the effects of society and relationships on fostering abuse. Different therapeutic schools and modalities approach abuse differently, from Freudian and Jungian, which involve interior reflection and discovery, through more behaviorally oriented approaches, which may not look back into the past very much at all as the therapist helps catalyze change and growth.

Recovery involves the need to address all dimensions where the wound has left a mark. Having support helps us manage the potentially overwhelming work of finding and juggling care. The challenge we face is that we have experienced ruptured relationships and failures in trusted authority. Any health care and a trial-and-error approach require trusting authority in the professionals consulted. Even relying on family, friends, or social workers for support requires trusting individuals to be there and not to abandon someone. That is quite a stretch, especially to make at the beginning of recovery. There is no doubt. This is a conundrum in the early days of recovery, and it is so difficult that some people get stuck here and find it hard to progress.

There is no guarantee this process won't be hurtful from time to time. All these people will fall short. Why? Because they are people. The goal is to minimize the ways we can be undermined by how these failures will distress us in our early steps. Sometimes, we need to pace the process, move forward slowly, build one new professional or support person at a time. It means recovery takes longer, but it also means recovery can proceed without great distress.

Another way is to diversify support. Aside from healthcare, we have other support people. All of them will have other obligations. Those obligations will mean they are not available all the time. That is why a network of support helps. Several people as confidantes help spread the burden. Knowing some people may be helpful driving or doing errands or being company for a walk or a concert—and only some are the confidante who hears more about the struggle— is a way to have an even broader network of support. This is an important way to preserve relationships. Abuse ruptured relationships at an earlier point in life, but its effects on us now can add burden to relationships with people who want to help.

In the end, the burden for healing resides solely with us. No one else can fully carry that burden. It gets at the heart of the injustice of abuse. We who were 100% innocent of the harm done remain 100% responsible for our healing. Redress or remuneration may help relieve the burden, but the burden is still ours. That affects our relationships. We need to build a way to get support that does not expect someone to be our savior. A network of support keeps us in the driver's seat.

There remains one relationship that never fails and that is sufficient for all the pain you need to remember and process. The most important source of support often feels safe only last—a relationship with God. When all relationships of trust with authority are demolished in abuse, this relationship can be the one that survives. That is why this relationship is often the one that, in being the source of all the dimensions of every person, both takes the hit with us—and feels damaged, too.

This is where a relationship with a pastoral minister rounds out—and even grounds—all the other support. Here is where finding a path to a priest, in persona Christi, can be deeply healing, and it is worth all the time working with a pastoral minister to help facilitate that meeting or those meetings. That's why I do what I do.

As a postscript: This is also why only the most authentic relationships between God and a pastoral minister or priest survive work with survivors of abuse, especially clergy abuse. We understand the practical efficacy of being able to make it to the foot of the Cross on behalf of someone else for it to help a survivor until that day he or she can recognize where they are standing and what it means in terms of hope and of new life.

RELATIONAL HEALING

M any people think of "relational healing" as romance. Many people imagine that, once they fall in love, their beloved will save them, complete them. For many people, falling in love is the solution to life's problems, but in life where suffering is ubiquitous a different kind of savior is needed.

This is not to contradict many survivors who found remarkable levels of healing in their marriages. The love of a patient and understanding spouse can go a long way to soothe the pain within. A new life with a healthy partner can create a world in opposition to the past and provide a sense of relief. Yet the pain is not fully soothed, and the past is not fully relieved through other people. That is our own work, whether we choose to do it or not. It's good to bear in mind that the loving spouse still suffers with their beloved and may bear unspoken burdens like the emotional isolation he or she can feel even when the survivor feels connected.

Yet there is no doubt that strong spouses, families, and other relationships can help us heal. There are remarkable healthcare workers and mentors and others we will meet. There is the pastoral minister or priest we will encounter. These are part of a milieu of healing, and some may become part of our stable network of support. In whatever healing that happens between two people, there can be the ripple effect outward to others, sometimes many people. What heals, even in marriages, is found in the very nature of friendship. And the impact of friendship, with all its courtesies and mutual respect, can be felt far and wide.

Friendship is a gift. For all people, friendship is a process of consciously choosing if (and when) to move closer to another person. For survivors of abuse, this process can be fraught with weathering the headwinds from the enduring and false lessons which abuse taught us. They are lessons which were and remain reasonable for us to believe.

Friendships in Christ are gifts of an Eternal proportion. They have a higher risk, because failure in a setting whose sense of safety is linked to faith in Jesus Christ not only ruptures a connection in human terms but can—and often does—rupture a sense of safety with the very Person Who is the ultimate safety now and forever.

Friendships can be channels of grace, some more than others, some not at all. There are even some that foster a most improbable healing. The therapeutic relationship has many dimensions. One is a kind of friendship, between albeit non-equal roles as a friendship between men- tor and protégé or between minister and youth can also be. Relationships even between people whose roles are not an equal stature can be friendships, can be particularly healing. So too with clergy.

Friendships between survivors and clergy, I believe are friendships that offer a restorative element for everyone in some measure. As if by proxy, a wholesome connection with a priest can restore to some degree, in some way those relationships with the Church and, more importantly, with God which were ruptured by abuse perpetrated by a different priest at a different time in life. They also help priests, who have been wounded by false associations with predators, heal.

Readers who aspire to support survivors of clergy abuse in a spiritual path toward healing that my reference to the centrality of clergy in this process is not excluding you. Let's take a moment to remember that we have each of us been chosen to be a royal priesthood, to be a holy nation, to speak of how God called us each

out of darkness into His wonderful light.[4] Some
of us will have the privilege of accompanying a
person who is healing from abuse or trauma on
a spiritual level. It's likely our friendship with
them will be deeper and more regular than any
a priest can offer given the high demands on
priests in their sacramental role for the Church.
It will likely be our own personal experience
of darkness and agony that will be called into
service. It will likely be our ability to sustain
praise for the Way, the Truth, and the Light that
will be the testimony on which wounded people
rely. While we may not have the sacramental
role of an ordained priest, it will be each of us
whose relationship with Jesus will be tested. It
will be a sacrificial experience for each of us, for
we sacrifice some portion of our sense of security
when we witness the depravity that led to the
harm brought upon children and vulnerable

---

4. "But you are a chosen people, a royal priesthood, a holy nation, God's
special possession, that you may declare the praises of him who called you
out of darkness into his wonderful light." 1 Peter 2:9.

adults. We give up a sense of our own control because nothing teaches us powerlessness like witnessing the potentially lifelong impact of abuse on innocent people, whom we find were neglected and abandoned by so many people who might have saved them. In this story, which is a common thread for all stories of abuse, we have the full role of Christian witness, able not to look away from a wholly deeper reality of the Cross and required to have a whole new awareness of what the Resurrection looks like in the life of the abused. It is we who are called to step out of the boat defying the logic of the world so that we can take the risk of reaching for the hand of the Savior on ourselves yet again, until our friend who has been abused can quite reach across that distance.

These friendships in Christ are needed for survivors of all abuse, but especially by those abused within the Church. These friendships are needed by family members of victims be- cause they are wounded by a single degree of separation. These friendships are crucial with and within schools and parishes where abuse by clergy or others with authority in the Church has occurred. Indeed, abuse has a seismic impact, rupturing relationships throughout the whole social fabric and into many generations. This book offers ways to understand and address abuse to end the ripples of magnitude in individuals, families, parishes, and the Church.

"I kept encountering remarkable people who believed in something stronger than the evil that had secretly triumphed in my young life."

WHY A SPIRITUAL GUIDE?

Let's say the restlessness that ignited and drives the recovery process is your and my experience of a whisper from God. It may be helpful to explore He Who is whispering to you, this safe God, this God Who will not harm you. How can you do this as recovery is upending life as you have known it and as the paradigm of how you think and act is being transformed? It may be time to explore a safe and knowledgeable, even a trauma-informed, relationship with someone to help integrate your faith with your recovery program—what does that mean?

It's important to ask this question and understand its answer to avoid confusion later. Therapy and spiritual guidance are complementary but not interchangeable. They proceed in

127

parallel, conscious of each other and supportive, but distinct. A therapist is well-suited to
delve into the details of abuse, help order and
understand them, help integrate them into a
well, adult life. If you turn to people who are not
equipped to help you, sometimes they withdraw
because they are not qualified to help you and
are overwhelmed. Recovery inevitably poses
the question whether or not we are responsible
for how we share details of the abuse, and with
whom. While each of us make that decision
differently based on circumstances and opportunities, none of us can escape the reality that
we may traumatize others, even inadvertently.
There are choices to be made in our hearts about
boundaries we need to set—on ourselves.

One way to get the most from formal spiritual
guidance is to find ways to make the exchange
prayerlike when possible. One way to enrich a
close friendship or more casual fellowship which
fosters spiritual understanding is to leave the

psychological impact of abuse for therapy, and to focus on whatever may help you grow and thrive as you recover. If you turn for therapy to people who are suited only to be spiritual friends or guides, you will likely emerge disappointed, maybe even feeling awkward. Both these feelings can kick up shame and harm your connection with your spiritual guide. Conversely, a crisis of faith can be discussed in therapy, certainly, but spiritual guidance helps you tap into your relationship with God through the depth of the tradition of faith (and all it offers for you to work through the sense of abandonment and betrayal). Recovery, for me, was a quilt. Everyone was an important piece in the patchwork. A very close friend whom I eventually found was central. Support groups and reading were critical. Together, it took all of these to keep me wrapped in care while I grew well.

I wish I could say that there are plenty of options for survivors of abuse within the Church to find care. That is not the case. Many people have little exposure to this pastoral care, or, if they do, they are trained therapists, all of whom have training to offer great contributions to your healing but only some of whom cannot emerge from the clinical training to offer pastoral care. And many professionals to whom you may be referred are working in areas where bishops and others have delegated all care to clinicians so that the pastoral need is overlooked and goes unrecognized. This is not to say that there are not remarkable priests and pastoral ministers with all types of backgrounds who want sincerely to help. This book and all its related books are meant to help you explore integrating faith into your recovery—and to invite such a person into a healing dialogue for you and for them. As you both develop a friendship in Christ, you also heal many other ruptures on the spiritual realm. There are many graces to be found in this act of courage and sacrifice.

WHERE WE END

Surviving abuse can feel like a futile exercise. Caring for someone who is grappling with surviving abuse can inspire despair. Offering pastoral care to survivor or loved one will do one thing: prove how powerless we are when confronted with evil and its impact—and show us why we needed a Savior to come and redeem us. We cannot overcome the lasting wounds of abuse without His Cross.

These are mysterious things, lived by survivors and our loved ones. In the worst of the pain, it can be impossible to recognize our suffering as part of the Cross of Jesus. We can hear the words but cannot conceive of the consolation where pain does not end but is transformed. This work in pastoral ministry will remind you, day after day, of your insufficiency and of God's majesty and power over evil and its impact.

The most important thing to remember is that abuse is so terrible because it proves our powerlessness, and it remains shrouded in mystery. Not everything about any abuse will be fully known or understood. Seldom is any instance of abuse fully remembered by an individual or a family.

The reason faith is critical to recovering from abuse is seen here, too. Seeing with eyes of faith we see that we are not the ultimate power nor were we meant to be. We are creatures of an Almighty God. If we can come to engage with abuse in our own past or the past of others without recoiling from its deep pain and suffering, we do not need to fear our powerlessness. We do not need to be frustrated by or lost in its enduring mystery. Our God is all powerful and is a mystery who encompasses all mystery. We do not need to be a savior because Christ Jesus is the Savior of everyone. He has already defeated the causes that led to this suffering and to all suffering and all evil and death. We need only believe—and walk our own *Via Dolorosa*.

The Lord is close to the brokenhearted,

saves those whose spirit is crushed.[1]

1. Psalm 34:19

"Look boldly at abuse in all its dimensions if you want to find the full dimension of yourself without shame— of the person whom God created, an abuser harmed, and the one true Savior can lead into new life.**"**

AWARD-WINNING GO-TO REFERENCE

Veronica's Veil: A Christ-Centered Guide to Integrating Faith with Recovery for Adult Survivors of Child Sexual Abuse by Clergy is the award-winning go-to reference for offering spiritual support to adults who are trying to integrate their Christian faith and the treasury of Catholic traditions into recovering from sexual abuse in a faith setting. This book transforms encounters into turning points in healing from the spiritual impact of all abuse and trauma.

With over 175 essays on topics common in psychotherapy and other treatment, *Veronica's Veil* provides practical tips and inspiration for both individual reflection and healing dialogue, all gently guided by the spirituality of St. Francis de Sales.

THE VERONICA'S VEIL SERIES

First Steps:
Overcoming Early Obstacles
to Recovery from Abuse

The most courageous steps a survivor of abuse can take are the first steps toward healing. *First Steps* sheds light on these early obstacles, especially where the wound of abuse has hurt so deeply that it's hard to trust even God. *First Steps* speaks from lived experience finding and following a path forward in faith through healing. These reflections are for survivors and family members, who suffer the wounds of abuse by one degree of separation, but also for anyone who encounters survivors and families struggling through a process of recovering from abuse, especially in a faith setting.

Top Topics:
Revisiting Themes in Trauma Recovery
in a Faith Setting

Survivors of abuse share a rich treasury of recovery literature where common topics and themes recur. *Top Topics* has collected one survivor's reflections on these fundamental concepts, drawing from a lived experience healing from wounds inflicted in a faith setting. Written by a survivor of abuse by clergy, *Top Topics* takes a fresh look at recovery literature through the lens of faith to imagine the healing potential of Catholic traditions and devotions. *Top Topics* is an important addition to the library of survivors and their family members, who suffer the wounds of abuse by one degree of separation, and for all those who wish to help them along their path to recovery.

Turning Points:
Facing Decisive Junctures
in Recovery from Abuse

The arc of recovery, moving from victim to a person thriving despite suffering abuse, is marked by junctures that can define how each survivor's next phase of recovery—and entire life—will unfold. *Turning Points* identifies some important decision points in recovery from abuse and shares the wisdom gained by one survivor who found a course forward in faith through healing. *Turning Points* is written for survivors and family members, who suffer the wounds of abuse by one degree of separation, and for all those who wish to help them along their path to recovery.

Reconciliation with Faith:
Cultivating a Heart at Peace
with a Wounding Church

Reconciliation with Faith is a collection of essays about how the treasury of Catholic faith and devotions can help survivors of abuse heal. With a special emphasis on surviving abuse within the setting of faith, *Reconciliation with Faith* is a roadmap for people moving from suffering a wounded faith to a healing with faith. Written originally for survivors and family members, who suffer the wounds of abuse by one degree of separation, along with helpers like spiritual directors and pastors, *Reconciliation with Faith* is a reminder to Catholics who have lost a sense of how our faith offers the healing from wounds which the human failures and corruption in our institutions have inflicted.

See SpiritFire.Online or online retailers for additional books and references.

Spirit Fire is a Christian Restorative Justice Initiative founded by Luis A. Torres, Jr., and Teresa Pitt Green. As survivors of clergy abuse Luis and Teresa sought to foster dialogue among all persons hurt by abuse within the Roman Catholic Church and beyond. They have facilitated dialogue between survivors and their families, on one hand, and Church leadership. They have provided workshops, retreats, and support for review boards and for initiatives in dioceses and religious communities. Their support and pastoral care included survivors, family members, and clergy who experienced abuse in their personal lives. Luis passed away in March 2023 from cancer caused by his service at Ground Zero after 9/11. A fund has been established in his honor to sponsor survivors of abuse at retreats led by Teresa. For more information, see SpiritFire.Online.

ABOUT THE AUTHOR

Teresa Pitt Green is an international speaker, writer, and advocate who is dedicated to helping survivors, families, and the Catholic Church heal in the wake of broad-scale sexual abuse within the Church. To that end, Pitt Green is co-founder of Spirit Fire, a Christian restorative justice initiative which facilitates dialogue between survivors with their families and, on the other hand, clergy, ministers, and Church leaders. She was counted among founders of *The Healing Voices Magazine*, an online magazine promoting dialogue about recovery from abuse in a faith setting; after five years of publication, it was read throughout the English-speaking Catholic world. Pitt Green has served in various capacities in the fight against human trafficking, e.g., on the leadership team for the Northern Virginia Human Trafficking Task Force. Teresa has been working at the intersection of addiction and trauma for several years in ministry to men in residential programs. She continues now to serve full-time in her area of focus, working with survivors, families, clergy, ministries, and leadership to promote understanding and healing from abuse. She is a survivor of clergy abuse. In 2024, The Catholic University of America recognized Teresa Pitt Green's ministry by bestowing an honorary doctoral degree in humanities.

www.ingramcontent.com/pod-product-compliance
Lightning Source LLC
Chambersburg PA
CBHW060500280326
41933CB00014B/2809